THE *KEYS* TO GETTING PUBLISHED

THE *KEYS* TO GETTING PUBLISHED

ADRIANNE MARIE HALL

ANTHURIUM PUBLISHING LLC

"Where Writers Become Published Authors"

www.anthuriumpublishing.com

ANTHURIUM PUBLISHING LLC

710 SOUTH MYRTLE AVENUE
No. 293
MONROVIA, CALIFORNIA 91016

www.anthuriumpublishing.com

ISBN-13: 978-0-9897188-1-3
ISBN -10: 0989718816

Published and Printed in the United States of America.

THE *KEYS* TO GETTING PUBLISHED

As long as you are the sole and exclusive author of the work, or own and have full legal authority to the copyrights, trademarks, and trade names associated with the body of work, you can publish it.

What Type Of Book Or Project Do You Want To Publish?

FICTION

- Action or Adventure
- Erotica
- Fantasy
- Horror
- Romance
- Science Fiction
- Short Story
- Suspense or Thriller

NON-FICTION

- Art and Photography
- Cookbook
- Craft, Hobby, Do It Yourself Manual
- Memoir, Personal or Family History
- Poetry

THE *KEYS* TO GETTING PUBLISHED

START WITH AN EDITED MANUSCRIPT
QUERY LETTER
INTERIOR FORMATTING

FRONT / BODY / BACK MATTER

ISBN
COPYRIGHT PAGE BASICS
BOOK DESCRIPTION
AUTHOR'S BIO
AUTHOR'S HEAD SHOT
COVER DESIGN
PRICING YOUR BOOK
DISTRIBUTION
MARKETING
GETTING PAID
BOOKSIGNINGS
ANTHURIUM'S 5-STEP PROCESS
AUTHOR'S NOTE

"If you wish to be a writer, write." - Epictetus

TABLE OF CONTENTS

"Cut your manuscript ruthlessly but never throw anything away: it's amazing how often a discarded scene or description, which wouldn't fit in one place, will work perfectly later." **– Robert Harris**

START WITH AN EDITED MANUSCRIPT

- It is important to have your manuscript or publishing project reviewed and edited by a professional editor and or proofreader. If you can't go that route... have at least two or three other well-read individuals look over your work product for you. Don't be your own proofreader or editor. You'll be sorry when the errors stick out like beacons in your published work.

- Be mindful that book reviewers, copy editors and proofreaders can accidently change the meaning of what you have written by correcting your English when they over estimate their own knowledge of the subject matter. Always read the work product again with fresh eyes especially after it has been edited. Be on the look out for typos, grammatical errors, punctuation errors, misspelled words, incorrect words, and missing words.

- Don't just rely on the spell check or grammar features built into your word processing program to track down errors in your manuscript. Those are both very useful tools, but they are not foolproof.

- If you use headers or footers in your manuscript be sure to double check spelling. You don't want to find out after your book has been published that the header or footer contains errors. Headers and footers should not appear on pages that are supposed to be left blank.

- If you have a Table of Contents and/or an Index, review chapter titles for spelling errors.

- Captions should match up to their corresponding pictures and tables. Check them for errors.

- Make sure that notations such as ***"in the picture below"*** or ***"in the image above"*** are on the same page as the referenced image.

"Above all, a query letter is a sales pitch and it is the single most important page an unpublished writer will ever write. It's the first impression and will either open the door or close it. It's that important, so don't mess it up. Mine took 17 drafts and two weeks to write."

- Nicholas Sparks.

QUERY LETTER

If you are hoping to submit your manuscript to a traditional publishing house, check their guidelines for query submission. Independent publishing houses normally have their guidelines for manuscript submission or a query form available on their web sites.

- You would not show up at a job interview in shorts and flip-flops, nor would you attend a black-tie event dressed in jeans and tennis shoes. That said, your Query Letter should be written as though you were trying your best to make a great first impression.
- The letter should be typed on one page, with clean margins, and completely clear of any and all typos or mistakes.
- If using snail mail, the paper should be clean and of good quality. Use a nice letterhead if possible. Include a SASE (self-addressed stamped envelope) in order to insure that you receive a return reply.
- Know who you are sending the Query Letter to and address it accordingly. "To whom it may concern" or "Dear Sir or Madam" says that you were not interested enough in finding out the name of the correct agent or editor. Call the agency and ask. Sometimes you might have to make more than one call to obtain the name of the person to whom you need to submit the Query Letter. Take your work seriously if you expect anyone else to take it seriously by doing your homework.
- Start your letter with a brief introduction that includes the title of your book. You will need to include the word count and genre if it is a work of fiction. If it is a work of non-fiction explain what type of non-fiction it is.
- Your next paragraph (two if necessary) will be a brief description of the story. With fiction you need to announce your main character, what his/her problem is, and how they resolve it. With non-fiction, you have to start with your argument, explain how you will prove your argument, and then present your proof. Don't provide your own take on whether or not your book is good. Your assessment of your own book will not be taken seriously.
- Finally, your last paragraph is where you talk about yourself, including what your qualifications are for writing the book. Mention any writing awards or accolades that you have received.
- Conclude your Query by asking if you may submit your work for consideration. Then sign your name.

***"Design is not just what it looks like and feels like. Design is how it works."* – Steve Jobs**

INTERIOR FORMATTING

- Use the **mirror** option in ***Word*** so that your inner and outer margins are lined up correctly on both the left and right hand pages. You don't want your text to be too close to the top, bottom, inner or outer edges of the facing pages in your published book.

- Top and bottom margins can sometimes change as a result of **widows** - *a word or line of text from a paragraph, heading, list, table, or caption that extends to the top of the next page;* and **orphans** *- a word, a line of text, a heading or caption that sits at the bottom of a page while the rest of the text unit continues on to the next page.* Because it is not visually appealing, pages should not end with a single indented line, nor should they start with a single un-indented line. Most word processing applications provide an option to specify that at least two lines must remain together at the top and bottom of a page. In ***Word*** click on the **Page Layout** tab then open the **Paragraph** dialog box. Select the **Line and Page Breaks** tab and under **Pagination** make sure to select the **Widow/Orphan** check box.

- Most word processing software programs come with hundreds of great fonts. Nevertheless, for the interior pages of your book use a font style that will be easy on the eyes. For example, the following are just a few common interior book fonts:

Adobe Garamond / Caslon / Minion Pro / Palatino Linotype / Bodoni MT
Tahoma / Baskerville Old Face / Verdana/ Georgia.

- The fonts listed above were typed using a 12pt font size. Bold was not used at all. Not only is it a good idea to use an easy to read font, but the finished size matters as well. Interior font sizes most commonly range from 9pt to 12pt. You can use larger font sizes however doing so will take up more page room which could result in a published book that is larger and more expensive to print than anticipated.

- Using a point size of 10, here again are those same fonts:

Adobe Garamond / Caslon / Minion Pro / Palatino Linotype / Bodoni MT
Tahoma / Baskerville Old Face / Verdana/ Georgia.

INTERIOR FORMATTING

- In the world of publishing, word count matters.
  - **Micro Story** = 500 words
  - **Short Story** = 1500 to 10,000 words
  - **A single plot Short Story** with very few characters = 2000 to 2500 words
  - **Novella** = 20,000 to 40,000 words
  - **Novel** = 40,000 plus words. Usually contains many characters, subplots, locations, and a span of time.
- You will want to "Justify" your text so that your pages have a clean look along the left and right side margins.

Following is a list of the components that can make up the Front, Body, and Back Matter of a book. Not all components are always appropriate to use.

- **Half-Title page** - This page should only contain the title of your book and is normally the first page one sees when opening the cover.
- **Frontispiece** - An illustration on the page facing the Title page.
- **Title page** - This page lists the title, subtitle, author and publisher of the book.
- **Copyright page** - Usually found on the backside of the Title page and includes the copyright notice, book edition, publication information, printing history, cataloging data, legal notices and the ISBN.
- **Dedication** - self-explanatory
- **Epigraph** - A quotation that the author might wish to include that is appropriate to the work.
- **Table of Contents** - Lists all of the chapters and or divisions of the book as applicable.
- **List of Figures** - For excessive illustrations or pictures this page includes their titles, and page numbers where they occur in the book.
- **List of Tables** - This page is dedicated to tables and is used very similarly to the List of Figures
- **Forward** – This is normally a short letter or notation written, signed and dated by someone other than the author.
- **Preface** – Written by the author, and tells the reader how the story or book came to be.
- **Acknowledgments** – The author expresses gratitude to those who helped in the creation of the book.
- **Introduction** – The authors provides the reader with the purpose and goal of the book.
- **Prologue** – For fiction, this sets the scene for the story and is usually told in the voice of a character from the book.
- **Second Half-Title** – Used if the front matter is particularly extensive, and it should be identical to the first Half-Title page.

INTERIOR FORMATTING

- **Body** – The main text of the book.
- **Epilogue** - An ending piece that is either in the voice of the author or a continuation of the main narrative with a purpose of bringing closure to the story.
- **Afterward** - May be written by either the author or another designee and it deals with the origin of the work or seeks to place the work in a wider context or association.
- **Conclusion** - A short or brief summary of the main parts or arguments of the work.
- **Postscript**- An addition to or afterthought to the original body of work.
- **Appendix / Addendum** – A supplement to the main work, might include additional source materials that were not available during the pre-publishing process or were unable to be added to the original body of the work.
- **Chronology** - Used mostly in historical works and lists the events by date order. Might be similar to an Appendix or the author might choose to use it in the front matter if it is critical to the understanding of the work.
- **Notes** - Sometimes called Endnotes and they appear after the Appendices and before the Bibliography or List of Contributors.
- **Glossary** - Alphabetical list of terms and their definitions.
- **Bibliography** - A list of the books and periodicals that have been cited in the main body of the work.
- **List of Contributors** - Sometimes appears in the front matter, this lists all of the contributors to the body of work.
- **Index** - Alphabetical listing with page numbers of people, events, places , concepts, and works cited within the body of work.
- **Errata** - A notice from the publisher of an error in the book that was probably caused during the production process.
- **Colophon** - A notice at the end of a work describing the typography including typeface by name and its history. Might also include an acknowledgment of the book designer or other persons involved with the design and production of the book.

"For one who reads, there is no limit to the number of lives that may be lived, for fiction, biography, and history offer an inexhaustible number of lives in many parts of the world, in all periods of time." **- Louis L'Amour**

ISBN - ONE SIZE DOES NOT FIT ALL

ISBN 0-918894-28-X

00028

0 29129 00495

The barcode that you see on the back of a book is the scannable version of the ISBN

The International Standard Book Number aka ISBN, is a 13-digit number used to identify the publisher, author, title, and the specific edition of a book. Each ISBN is a unique number and can only be assigned once. ***They cannot be reused***. Booksellers, libraries, universities, wholesalers, and distributors use this number to order, price and keep track of inventory.

If you are going to sell your book to the public, every edition and format of your book will need its very own ISBN. For example, let's say that you have decided to publish your book in paperback, hardcover and e-book. Under this scenario you will need three unique ISBNs. When using the e-book format there are currently three publishing options available which are Kindle, ePub *(used by Nook, iBook, and almost all other e-book readers)*, and PDF *(used for art books, manuals, and instructional books)*. If you choose to publish in every format option currently available, you will ultimately need five ISBNs. If in the future you wish to publish a new edition of any pre-published format, you will need a new ISBN for that publication as well. Every book and e-book in the retail and wholesale market must have its own unique ISBN.

An individual ISBN currently costs $125.00. Publishers normally purchase them in bulk.

An ISBN is not actually required if you are publishing a book that will not be sold through any online store or brick and mortar retail or wholesale market; or if you only plan to sell the book personally at an event, presentation, talk, or conference; or if the book is going to be given away directly to a very controlled group like friends or family members.

"A lie can travel half way around the world while the truth is putting on its shoes." **– Charles Spurgeon**

COPYRIGHT PAGE BASICS

The copyright page follows the main title page of the book and is where the legal information is documented. Following is a sample of a basic copyright page. It is always a good idea to take a look at the copyright pages from a few books that fall under your genre or category to determine which elements might be necessary for your book.

- Book Title
- Author's Name
- Copyright © 2014 by (Publishing Company) and/or (Name of Author).
- All rights reserved, including the right to reproduce or scan this book or portions thereof in any form whatsoever without the prior written permission of (Name of Author) and or (Publishing Company) except where permitted by law.
- Publisher's address and contact information
- www.publisherswebsite.com
- ISBN-10: 0-0000000-0-0
- ISBN-13: 000-0-0000000-0-0
- Printed in the United States of America
- Include name credits for Cover or Book Design, Photos, Illustrations, Editing, etc.
- First Edition: (MM/YYYY)
- Limit of Liability / Disclaimers of Warranty

"Live out of your imagination, not your history."
- Stephen Covey

BOOK DESCRIPTION

The Book Description is one of the most difficult elements for authors to create, yet it is also one of the most important pieces needed in their arsenal of marketing materials. The process of writing the description can send shivers through to the bone of many authors because instinctually they don't want to leave out any of the details. But this is not the platform authors should use for re-telling the story that they are ready to publish. This is the platform authors use to get potential readers interested enough in the story to purchase it once it is published. Here are a few things to keep in mind when creating a book description:

- The description should be based solely on your main plot. Do not include subplots because that is just too much information.
- Try to keep your description under 150 words. Keep it simple... tell the potential reader in as few words as possible what your book is about. Think about your audience and why they should want to pick up your book.
- Your description should be told in the present tense, third person point-of-view. Envision that you are sitting across from a potential reader who just asked you to describe what your book is about. Write down what you would say to them. Be as intriguing in your brief description as possible. Keep it short and to the point. Don't give away your story. You've worked too hard to get published. Now let your readers purchase your book and read the story for themselves.
- When trying to write an intriguing description, you should use a few words that convey the same feelings or emotions that your book does. Think about the words that you might use to describe your book if you wrote comedy, horror, Sci-fi, murder, suspense etc. Don't oversaturate your description with too many emotionally descriptive words, you want to be strategic and deliberate with your delivery.
- You need to focus on making an impact on the person who is trying to decide whether or not they should purchase your book, instead of moving on to the next author's book. You only have a few seconds to get them interested, so use your head and not your heart.
- This book description will appear on the back cover of your book. It will also be part of your other printed publication announcements and will be used on web sites, social media outlets, and will sometimes accompany your Author's Bio. ***Yes, you need to write an Author's Bio too.***

"I love those who can smile in trouble, who can gather strength from distress, and grow brave by reflection. 'Tis the business of little minds to shrink, but they whose hearts are firm, and whose conscience approves their conduct, will pursue their principles unto death."

- Leonardo da Vinci

AUTHOR'S BIO

When it comes to creating an author's biography, the best advice is to have more than one in your arsenal. As a matter of fact, you should prepare several that vary in word count and detail. Starting with twenty-five words in length, use that as a foundation to create one that is fifty words in length (which might possibly go into a query letter). For a press release, book signing, or even a writer's conference a bio can range from 100 to 500 words in length so develop them in ways that allow you to add to or edit down in order accommodate the length needed. Sometimes an author will be asked to submit a bio for use in an article or other publication. For such requests, inquiring about word count is always a good idea. It can be far easier to write a novel than to write one's own biography. Consider the process that one might use for creating a character and use that same process to develop several layers to the author's biography. Using a little writer's creativity, answering any one or combination of the following questions can help with the development of a bio in any length.

- What is your back story?
- Where do you come from?
- What makes your background special or unique?
- Did your childhood experiences help to shape your writing style?
- When did you first decide to start writing?
- When did you become interested in the subject matter of your book?
- Where did you get your idea for the book?
- Where did you get your ideas for the characters in your book?
- Do you personally relate to any character in the story?
- Can you personally relate to the story?
- If it directly relates to the story line or subject matter of your book, it might be appropriate to mention how your personal background, education or professional experience validates how or why you have expertise with the theme, topic or content of your book.

"There are no rules for good photographs, there are only good photographs." **- Ansel Adams**

AUTHOR'S HEADSHOT

In a world where people are always snapping pictures using their cell phones, it isn't necessary to run out and spend a lot of money on professional head shots unless that is your preference. It is however a very good idea to have a few clear high resolution images of yourself on hand. Your image will appear on the back of your book, on promotional materials, and anything that needs to represent you as an author including online media. Here are some suggestions:

- The image should focus specifically on your face.
- Choose a 5″x 7″ image with a resolution of no less than 1224 x 1632 at 300dpi. The megapixel rating should not be less than 2.0. The larger the megapixel rating the larger the options are for print size.
- Most cell phone images have a picture resolution of 1195 x 1600 or larger. So if you don't have a point-and-shoot or other digital camera but you do have a cellphone that can take great pictures, you should be just fine.
- Don't use an image that is more than four years old especially if your appearance has changed dramatically.
- JPEG images are incredibly versatile and are easily imported into a multitude of software programs. This is the standard format of a picture taken with a cellphone. If you do use a point-and-shoot or digital camera you should save your images into a JPEG format.
- If you have to go out and take photos, choose a background setting that is clean and uncomplicated.
- Clothing should not be busy but complimentary to your hair color. If you have light hair wear dark clothing. If you have dark hair wear lighter clothing. Don't wear busy prints.
- You don't want to wear anything that will distract from your face. Stay clear of large jewelry pieces or hats.
- Never take a picture if you are tired because those bags under your eyes will show up like beacons in a photo.
- Most importantly, have fun and enjoy the process.

"Design is the method of putting form and content together. Design, just as art, has multiple definitions; there is no single definition. Design can be art. Design can be aesthetics. Design is so simple, that's why it is so complicated." **- Paul Rand**

COVER DESIGN

Most often the last thing on an author's mind is the design of their book cover. That said, an attention grabbing cover might be one of their best marketing assets. In reality people at times will judge whether or not they should invest any interest at all in a book because of its cover. Visual communication is subjective and there is a fine line to presenting a cover that conveys the essence or feeling of a book without giving away a literal taste of it. You want potential readers to be curious about your story and read it. You don't want to tell the story on the cover.

The best advice for any author is to remember that the book cover is as important to the outside of the book as a professionally edited manuscript is to the inside. Writers work on their craft for years to master their unique styles. Graphic artists and designers do the same. If you are a writer and graphic design is not your forte, hire a graphic designer to create your book cover. The cost might range anywhere from $100 to $500 but if your book is worth publishing at all, it is worth publishing well with a skillfully designed cover.

Don't expect a designer to read your manuscript. It is important that you provide them with enough information to insure that the two of you see eye to eye on what emotions or feelings you wish to convey with your book. Talk about colors or images that you would like for them to consider using. Images are not always necessary for good cover design. Sometimes your title is enough and the design can center around the creative use of text. Look at other book covers including those in your own collection and make a note of those that catch your eye and why they interest you. This information can be invaluable to your designer.

"There is only one boss. The customer. And he can fire everybody in the company from the chairman on down, simply by spending his money somewhere else."
– Sam Walton

PRICING YOUR BOOK

Under "Interior Formatting" it was mentioned that interior font sizes normally range from 9pt. to 12pt. Using a larger font size can ultimately result in a thicker or larger book than anticipated. When publishing an e-book this might not be an issue. However when using Print-On-Demand (POD) this can result in a higher per unit print cost.

POD is a dream come true for independently published authors. Instead of having to set aside storage space for cases of books, they can order only the amount of books that they need and when they need them. Knowing the POD costs along with factoring in tax and shipping will help the author decide on an accurate wholesale and retail price point for their book.

A few of the elements that factor into the POD cost of a single book are as follows:

- **Trim size** (book size).

  Trade paperbacks are normally between 5½″ x 8½″ to 6″ x 9″. However memoirs and short stories are oftem 5¼″ x 8″. Manuals, photo books, and workbooks are larger and range from 8″ x 8″ to 8 ½″ x 11″. Mass market books which are sold through point of purchase sites like supermarkets and airports are normally 4¼″ x 7″.

- **Font Style and Font Size** really does matter. The measurements below are based on using an 8½″ x 11″ sheet of typed paper.

Times New Roman Font Size	10	12	14	16	20
Maximum anticipated words per page	1112	815	582	435	320
Lines per page - *in order to obtain this quantity, it will be necessary to adjust the page margins for your entire manuscript.*	60	50	43	37	33

PRICING YOUR BOOK

- **Final Page Count**

  Font style and size determine the number of words that can be typed on a regular 8½″ x 11″ page. To estimate what the final page count will be for a standard paperback, it is probably more helpful to use a ratio of three published paperback pages to one typed 8½″ x 11″ page. Of course when dealing with the front matter section of a book, this ratio of published pages to typed pages will not be the same. Refer to the section on "Interior Formatting" which lists those dedicated front matter pages.

- **Binding Styles**

  There are many binding styles to choose from, and finding the best one for your book is an important part of the publishing process. The standard binding style for most paperback books is called **Perfect Binding.** This is possibly the most cost effective binding method used by POD shops. **Saddle Stitching** is the method of stapling the book at the spine fold and is popular for thin poetry books, instruction manuals, playbills and children's books. **Spiral Binding** is popular with larger books like workbooks, cookbook, and educational literature that work best when open flat. **Plastic Comb** is used most often for binding proposals, instructional manuals, and educational materials. **Hard Cover** is probably the most expensive binding style and can most often be used for large medical or business books, and coffee table books.

PRICING YOUR BOOK

- The type of paper used in printing your interior pages, as well as using special or protective coating on the book cover can also factor into the final cost of your POD book.

- Keeping track of your bottom line costs is important. However in order to stay competitive in the retail market, you need to be in tune with the price range of books that are in your genre. The consumer is not at all concerned with your print costs but you can be mindful of the things that can cause your POD costs to be elevated, which will cut into your profit margin.

- A novel that is around 350 to 375 pages in length could reasonably be priced at $16.95. This is competitive in the retail market when you consider that the average price of a paperback novel falls between $13.95 and $17.95. The industry standard wholesale discount is 55% off retail and if your POD cost is $6 or more per unit, this can really sting and eat into your profits.

"The purpose of a business is to create a customer."
– Peter Drucker

DISTRIBUTION

- Now is a wonderful time to be an indie author. This distinction also comes with the flexibility to be creative and experimental with where and how you choose to distribute your title .

- Online stores like Amazon are popular because of their ease of use and immediate access. Buyers no longer have to travel to a physical bookstore to make purchases. By exerting only as much energy as it takes to click a mouse or tap a finger, any device capable of accessing the internet can be used as a portal for purchasing books. With fairly reasonable shipping costs, physical books can be mailed or shipped to any address a purchaser chooses in a matter of a day or two. Having a print book listed with an online bookstore allows access to your title by millions of readers all over the world.

- Nothing is more amazing than being able to immediately download a purchased e-book like those sold through Amazon for the Kindle. None Kindle owners can purchase and download Kindle e-books by installing the free Kindle installer program on their PC, Mac, I Pad, Nook, or cellphone. Other online bookstores also carry their own dedicated e-reader. More than likely by doing a fairly simple internet search, anyone can locate third-party e-reader software programs that can be installed on just about any digital device, making the e-book an accessible format for everyone. Having your e-book available in multiple formats increases your potential to reach more readers.

- As an indie author you can and should offer your book for sell through a dedicated web site. Have business cards with your name and book web site with you at all times. It is always a good idea to have a few extra copies of your title on hand for direct to public sales and impromptu book signings. No it is not vain to carry a copy or two of your book around in your trunk. Nor is it vain to tell people that you are an author. You are probably going to be your entire marketing team so plug your accomplishment whenever you can.

"There are no secrets to success. It is the result of preparation, hard work, and learning from failure."
– Colin Powell

MARKETING

Thanks to the internet and social media, getting the word out about your new book can be as simple as dedicating a few moments a day to a few hours a week sitting at your computer.

- One of the first things you should do is have a web site set up for your book with a dedicated web site address "www.thenameofmybook.com". Share the link with everyone you know. If possible set up a shopping cart or PayPal feature whereby fans can purchase an autographed copy of your book directly from you. If your book is available at online retailers like Amazon include a direct link from your web site to that retailer so that visitors can purchase your book from them as well.
- Host a contest or drawing and offer a free signed copy of your book as the prize.
- Post special offers to book clubs in the area. If they choose your book to add to their must read list, offer to attend one of their club meetings where you can sign everyone's copy.
- If you are on Facebook or LinkedIn you should use those platforms to announce the release of your book. If you feel that it will be helpful, create a separate Facebook account to promote your book. Join author and writing groups on LinkedIn. Get involved with the discussions and see what's current in the world of writing.
- Do some internet research for publications, web sites, blogs, on line newsletters, and news groups that fit your target audience or genre. Find out how you might be able to contribute commentary or participate in discussions.
- Create a media packet which includes a press release, cover shot of your book and its description, your author's bio and headshot. You never know when an opportunity will arise for you to promote yourself and your book. Keep a digital file and several hard copies.
- Encourage reviews and feedback from your fans. You can post these quotes on your book's web site and include them in your media kit. Fans can also leave feedback at online retailer sites regarding your book.

Stay engaged in the process. Keep learning because nothing happens overnight when it comes to publishing a book, book sales or being validated as an author. It can take months, or it can take years. If writing is your passion, stay focused and do it because of the enjoyment that you get out of it. If being rich is your focus, then you might want to try doing something else.

"Money won't create success, the freedom to make it will."
- Nelson Mandela

GETTING PAID

- In traditional publishing there are two common payment structures for authors. The first is a flat fee, which is sometimes divided into two 50% payments - one being an advance against future anticipated royalties and the second being paid out upon receipt of a final manuscript. If the book sells above and beyond what is expected, the author receives additional royalty checks down the line. If the book does not sell as expected, the publishing house loses money.

- The second payment method is for a traditional publishing house to pay royalties to an author based on a percentage of actual sales. Under this scenario stores purchase books from the publisher at a 30-50% discount off the retail price. The publisher then pays the author up to 10% of the net or retail profits for a hardcover book, and up to 8% of the net or retail profits for a paperback. The publisher decides whether they pay using the net rate or the retail rate.

- Book packagers who deal with mass market books, sometimes work with collaborating authors and pay them a flat fee from the proceeds of book sales. In this scenario, fees are also paid out to the entire team that helped with the book which would include copywriters, illustrators, proofreaders, editors and marketing, etc.

- The independent publishing world is set up so that indie authors receive all of the proceeds from their book sales. These authors are much more involved with the process of publishing their books, and deciding what expenses they will incur. Online booksellers like Amazon pay royalties directly to the author for their online print and e-book sales. They also offer a variety of selling options and additional marketing outlets that authors can access. The royalties from e-books can be slightly higher than those from paperbacks, which is why some indie authors choose to publish e-books only.

"If you have a positive attitude and constantly strive to give your best effort, eventually you will overcome your immediate problems and find you are ready for greater challenges." **- Pat Riley**

BOOK SIGNINGS

So your book is now published and you can officially call yourself a published author. Armed with your new release, you are anxiously dreaming about lines of fans wanting an autographed copy. You are probably even practicing your autograph signature. The truth of the matter is, it takes some pre-planning, post production and a lot of creativity to launch a successful book signing.

- You will want to make sure that you have a system in place to accept credit card payments. These days you can do this with your cellphone and a card reader. For example check out the Square or PayPal. The Square transfers funds directly into a pre-designated bank account within 48 hours of received payments. PayPal deposits funds into your PayPal account. You have to go into that account later and transfer funds over to your pre-designated bank account. Both systems offer a free card reader and the fees for using their service is a small percentage of the payments received.

- People still pay with cash so have a cash box and the ability to make change. Ideally, having someone with you who can take care of processing payments is best, because you will want to focus on your fans.
- Always have a supply of your books on hand well in advance of a book-signing.
- Order promotional materials that you can give away. Bookmarks are always appropriate.
- Use your online network, and contact lists to let people know about an upcoming book signing.
- Plan ahead and choose your venue location wisely. Know the layout of the room before the big day if possible.
- As dedicated bookstores start to disappear, think out of the box and consider partnering with a venue that relates to your book. For a craft book contact a hobby shop; for a DIY book contact a building supply store. Don't forget those mom and pop shops where you do business. Ask them if they wouldn't mind hosting a book signing for you. Look for area businesses that are supportive of local authors and artists. If you have a cookbook, consider setting up at a farmer's market. A friends home would be great for demonstrating a recipe or special cooking technique that you feature in your book. As a matter of fact, in home book signings are fantastic venues for hosting an RSVP event. Have some light munchies, fruit and wine for your guests. People love feeling invited to something special.
- Be prepared to talk a bit about your book. This is where your book description can come in handy. Have a question and answer period. Fans love to feel like they can connect one on one with an author.
- Your signing table or greeting area should be inviting. Cover your table with a nice cloth and place a plant or vase of fresh flowers on it. If you can, display a poster or banner with an image of your book cover on it. And last but not least, it's always nice to have a bowl of wrapped candy at your table for your fans.

ANTHURIUM PUBLISHING LLC

5 - STEP PUBLISHING PROCESS

We use an easy-to-understand **5-Step** publishing process which includes a consultant assigned to each of our clients to work with them one-on-one from the beginning to the end of their publishing journey. Please check out our web site at **www.anthuriumpublishing.com** to find out more about our publishing model and what we can do for you.

- **Step 1- Initial Inquiry and Query Letter** – We have an easy to complete on-line Query Letter form that can be submitted directly from the web site.
- **Step 2- Publishing Packages & Invoicing** – We currently offer five budget conscious publishing package options. Along with those options our clients can elect to purchase additional customized services.
- **Step 3- Review, Sign & Return Agreement with Payment** – All of our services are clearly documented and invoiced for our clients to review and approve before they pay for them.
- **Step 4- Checklist For Submitting Your Manuscript & Related Files** – Publishing a book should be a wonderful experience from start to finish. Because we want our clients to enjoy the process, their experienced consultant will provide knowledgeable assistance and guidance through-out the entire publishing process.
- **Step 5- Proofs & The Final Book Review Process** – We take the review of final proofs very seriously. Before a manuscript makes its published debut, we want our clients to be confident that they have put in all of the time necessary and exhausted every opportunity possible in order to present the best version of their book to the world.

Where writers become published authors

Anthurium Publishing LLC provides the synthesis for writers to translate their creative ideas into professionally-published works; converting truth, fiction, poetic thoughts and expertise into a recorded legacy to be read, savored and shared.

www.anthuriumpublishing.com

AUTHOR'S NOTE

My first published novel "Thresholds" was born from an eighteen year old manuscript that I wrote when my three children were very young. For over a decade and a half I thought of going the independent publishing route with the manuscript but I kept putting that endeavor off because the time just never seemed to be right. Then after years of re-writing and re-editing the manuscript, I finally sent it to a publisher. Within a few months a box arrived with the first printed copies of my published novel. With nearly two decades of work that had been invested from start to finish, my adult daughter dubbed the novel her youngest sibling. It was exciting and incredibly surreal to see the results of pages and pages of my writing finally packaged and finished so beautifully into a bound book. However the road that I traveled with the publisher from manuscript to novel was not at all free of potholes. Because there are so many moving parts to the publishing process, not being made aware of them at the start of the journey could prove to be discouraging and or overwhelming while on the path to getting published. When I decided that my plans were to continue writing with the expectation of publishing my work, I knew it was time to move full speed ahead and invest as much time and energy as necessary into learning the ins and outs of the world of independent publishing. I was determined to streamline the process and make it more enjoyable not just for my future self, but for other writers who dream of being published authors as well. The Keys To Getting Published combines years of research and experience into a handbook that is easy-to-read and understand by any writer who wishes to become a published author. Regardless of where you are on your writing and publishing journey I truly hope that The Keys To Getting Published provides you with the information needed to help you proceed smoothly toward your ultimate goal.

Happy Writing – Adrianne Marie Hall

adrianne@anthuriumpublishingllc.com
info@anthuriumpublishing.com
http://www.anthuriumpublishing.com

www.ingramcontent.com/pod-product-compliance
Lightning Source LLC
LaVergne TN
LVHW070154110826
845147LV00002B/399

* 9 7 8 0 9 8 9 7 1 8 8 1 3 *